Cannelle et Vanille

NOTES

Aran Goyoaga

Toss pitted cherries and sliced apples, pears, rhubarb, or peaches (any favorite fruit that will withstand baking) with maple syrup or orange juice, vanilla, and cinnamon. Place on a baking sheet, dot with butter, and roast at 400 degrees F until softened. Serve with crunchy granola and creamy yogurt.

Slice long, thin strips of rhubarb and toss with a tablespoon or two of sugar and the zest from an orange (maybe even a drop of orange blossom extract). Roll out your favorite pie dough and sprinkle a handful of almond flour in the center. Pile the rhubarb on top, then gently fold the dough edges over it, leaving the center exposed. Bake at 425 degrees F for 40 minutes, or until golden brown.

Turmeric

Onion Skin

Beet

Blueberry

Rooibos
Hibiscus

Hibiscus

Make a fragrant light syrup: over medium heat in a small pot, combine 1 cup water, ⅓ cup sugar, and a split vanilla bean with seeds. When the sugar dissolves, add 3 cups sliced rhubarb and cook for a couple minutes, until it is soft and lightly stains the syrup. Cool slightly, then toss in other summer fruits and mix gently until they glisten. The topping is luscious over panna cotta, thick yogurt, or ice cream.

Radicchio, shaved fennel, pan-roasted radishes, canned sardines, toasted sunflower seeds, microgreens, olive oil, squeeze of lemon, and sea salt.

A simple cheese board always pleases a crowd. Have a variety of cheeses based on milk type: sheep, goat, and cow. Offer a selection of hard aged cheeses, soft creamy ones, and veiny blues. There should also be something sweet, such as a fruit jam, quince paste, or scattered fruit. Ideally nuts too—walnuts and hazelnuts are nice options.

Over medium heat, melt a good dab of butter in a skillet, then sprinkle in some sugar and squeeze in the juice of an orange. Place halved pears in the pan and cook until caramelized. Serve with a dollop of cream and a drizzle of the hot caramel.

Drizzle a variety of root vegetables with olive oil, and sprinkle with salt, pepper, ground cumin, and chili powder. Roast on a baking sheet at 400 degrees F until golden brown, about 30 minutes. Turn off the oven for another 5 minutes to further soften.

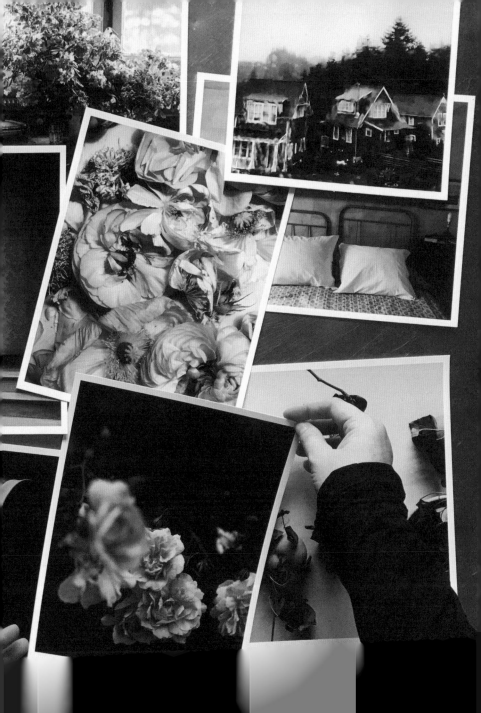

A thin sliver of warm chocolate cake with a soft dollop of cream and a shot of amaro. Nothing more needed.

Reflections

MANDARINS

As a child, winter meals ended
with the skins of mandarin
oranges scattered all over the
tablecloth. Citrus: nature's candy
during the quiet season, giving us
just what we need.

NATURA MORTA

Lady Emma Hamilton roses bloom in my garden from May through November. I speak to them in the early morning, as someone once told me they are listening. I take enormous pleasure in the discipline of deadheading and pruning them—and oh, what beauty they give.

THE FEEL OF A KITCHEN

In my home, I crave the feeling of warm wood, rough linen, wool, imperfect ceramics, and worn metals. Objects that come with a story, that are passed down through generations, are the ones that carry the spirit. My father's paintings are displayed in abundance and inspire my work more than I could have ever anticipated. I say, make room for objects that move you.

BREAKFAST INSPIRATION

Toss pitted cherries and sliced apples, pears, rhubarb, or peaches (any favorite fruit that will withstand baking) with maple syrup or orange juice, vanilla, and cinnamon. Place on a baking sheet, dot with butter, and roast at 400 degrees F until softened. Serve with crunchy granola and creamy yogurt.

DAHLIAS

Dahlias are the last statement flower that carries us from summer into autumn. Café au Lait is the large dusty pink-brown that I covet.

RHUBARB GALETTE

Slice long, thin strips of rhubarb and toss with a tablespoon or two of sugar and the zest from an orange (maybe even a drop of orange blossom extract). Roll out your favorite pie dough and sprinkle a handful of almond flour in the center. Pile the rhubarb on top, then gently fold the dough edges over it, leaving the center exposed. Bake at 425 degrees F for 40 minutes, or until golden brown.

FLOWERS OVER AN OLD SINK

I once taught a workshop at Kimbri Farm and art studio in the Blue Mountains of Australia. The rose bushes and bundles of flowering tree branches around their home became the subject of many photographs, including over this sink. The art studio was home for just a few days, but the hospitality and beauty were inspiration for years to come.

CARROTS

In late winter or early spring, I decide what vegetables I will plant in the garden. I always include small, stubby carrots. It's their strange curves that make them so beautiful and photogenic. I toss them into salads and roasts and they are sweet and delicious, but really I plant them because I admire their imperfect beauty.

ZUCCHINI BLOSSOMS

The fragrant, delicate flowers of zucchini and summer squash are wonderful gems of nature. Top a salad with thin slices of the raw blossoms or add to an omelet or pizza. Stuff them whole with soft cheese and fry them in a light tempura.

DYED EGGS

Celebrate spring. Leaves, flowers, fruits, and vegetables create beautiful natural dyes. Bring 4 cups water, 2 tablespoons white vinegar, and 4 cups chopped vegetables or ¼ cup tea leaves or ground spices (see color options to right) to a boil in a deep pot. Reduce heat to low, add 4 eggs, and simmer for about 25 minutes, or until the desired hue is achieved.

Yellow—Ground turmeric

Orange—Yellow onion skin

Deep orange—Yellow and red onion skins

Pink—Chopped red beets

Bright blue—Blueberries

Darker blue—Red cabbage

Smoky navy blue—Hibiscus tea leaves

Brown—Rooibos tea leaves

Dark slate gray—Rooibos and hibiscus tea leaves

RANUNCULUS

On Sunday mornings I visit our farmers' market religiously and scout the stalls before it opens. Ranunculus in the spring are a favorite. They are kept away from direct sun, as their delicate stems can easily wither. The unpretentious way they are bundled together in plain buckets always draws me in. It's their wild beauty I admire.

FRUIT TOPPING

Make a fragrant light syrup: over medium heat in a small pot, combine 1 cup water, ⅓ cup sugar, and a split vanilla bean with seeds. When the sugar dissolves, add 3 cups sliced rhubarb and cook for a couple minutes, until it is soft and lightly stains the syrup. Cool slightly, then toss in other summer fruits and mix gently until they glisten. The topping is luscious over panna cotta, thick yogurt, or ice cream.

TOMATOES FROM THE GARDEN

Sliced ripe tomatoes with a drizzle of olive oil and a sprinkle of salt—and toasted bread to soak up all the juices—is all I want to eat in the summer.

SIMPLE RADICCHIO SALAD

Radicchio, shaved fennel, pan-roasted radishes, canned sardines, toasted sunflower seeds, microgreens, olive oil, squeeze of lemon, and sea salt.

CHEESE

A simple cheese board always pleases a crowd. Have a variety of cheeses based on milk type: sheep, goat, and cow. Offer a selection of hard aged cheeses, soft creamy ones, and veiny blues. There should also be something sweet, such as a fruit jam, quince paste, or scattered fruit. Ideally nuts too—walnuts and hazelnuts are nice options.

APPLES

I never tire of photographing apples, especially those from unkempt, wild trees. I'm drawn to their spotty skins, unruly leaves, and even lichen on branches in dire need of pruning. Their texture embodies the poetry of nature.

CARAMELIZED PEARS

Over medium heat, melt a good dab of butter in a skillet, then sprinkle in some sugar and squeeze in the juice of an orange. Place halved pears in the pan and cook until caramelized. Serve with a dollop of cream and a drizzle of the hot caramel.

ROASTED ROOT VEGETABLES

Drizzle a variety of root vegetables with olive oil, and sprinkle with salt, pepper, ground cumin, and chili powder. Roast on a baking sheet at 400 degrees F until golden brown, about 30 minutes. Turn off the oven for another 5 minutes to further soften.

DISPLAY YOUR WORK

Hang your own art. Display it proudly. Take time for a creative practice, whatever that may be for you. It nourishes the soul.

TO END A MEAL

A thin sliver of warm chocolate cake with a soft dollop of cream and a shot of amaro. Nothing more needed.

FISHERMEN'S TERMINAL

I will always live where the water meets the fog.

THE CARE PACKAGE

My friend Terisa lives on an orchard in Southern California and sends me an annual care package filled with persimmons, avocados, all kinds of citrus, herbs, rose petals, candied fruit, and more. Terisa might not realize how much her generosity fills me with joy; sometimes it can be nearly impossible to comprehend the impact we have on others.

SOURDOUGH BREAD

Baking sourdough bread is the most grounding practice in my life. I have nursed my yeast starter for years, always watching it to see what it needs and how it responds. From it I bake nourishing loaves that keep me feeling connected. Tending to it is a commitment, but what it gives back is priceless.

CERAMICS

Handmade, one-of-a-kind ceramics are the only thing I collect. I seek out these objects that will make my food even more alive and beautiful.

BEAUTY IN DECAY

Capturing dying blooms is
tremendously emotional to me.
Perhaps it is a reminder of the
impermanence of everything.
I turn to nature in moments
when I need affirmation that
beauty and decay can coexist.

FLATWARE

I scavenge flea markets and
estate sales for old flatware
with its patina and history.
Mismatched utensils and
tableware add ease and
character to the table.

Aran Goyoaga is a cookbook author, food
stylist, and photographer. She was raised in the Basque
Country, in northern Spain, in a family of pastry chefs.
Her blog *Cannelle et Vanille* is a two-time James Beard
Award finalist. She lives in Seattle with her husband and
two children.

———————————————————————

Printed in China

SASQUATCH BOOKS with colophon is a registered
trademark of Penguin Random House LLC

25 24 23 22 21 20   9 8 7 6 5 4 3 2 1

Editor: Susan Roxborough
Production editor: Bridget Sweet
Designer: Anna Goldstein

ISBN: 978-1-63217-341-6

Sasquatch Books
1904 Third Avenue, Suite 710
Seattle, WA 98101

SasquatchBooks.com